Leonardo da Vinci by Ernest Raboff

Art for Children

The cover picture illustrates Leonardo's love of architecture and the human figure, only two subjects from his immense range of interests. Below, another is revealed in the three masterly studies of horses. Leonardo passionately admired their strength, beauty and nobility and, perhaps, no one before or since has so perfectly expressed their nature.

Whatever Leonardo undertook, he did with total commitment. For him, it was unthinkable to depict merely the outsides of things, without first having a thorough knowledge of their inner structure. The precision, power and beauty of all his work came from his deep understanding of all living things and his profound love and reverence for them.

Some 10,000 drawings from Leonardo's many sketchbooks can be seen in museums throughout the world. He was left-handed and always wrote in 'mirror' script in which sentences are written from right to left and the letters of the words are back to front.

Studies of Horses   Royal Collection, Windsor   **Head of Horse   Royal Collection, Windsor**

Detail: The Annunciation   Uffizi Gallery, Florence

THE AUTHOR

Ernest Raboff, artist, art critic, and art dealer, has been associated with art and artists for forty years.

As a young poet, he studied art in France and Italy, where he came in contact with Picasso, Léger, and the sculptor Giacometti. From Paris, Raboff travelled to Sweden where he lectured on the art of the United States. His illustrated book of poetry received a special award as Book of the Year in Sweden.

Mr Raboff has travelled to and studied in most of the great museums of the world, including the Tate and the National Gallery, the Uffizi, the Prado, the Louvre, the Jerusalem International, the Rijksmuseum, and the National Museum of Stockholm. Over the years working as a writer interested in art, a collector and an art dealer, he has become well-known to the international art community. His greatest pleasure is to guide children through the magic world of art and artists.

$$\frac{ZX}{1}$$

Dedicated to Kate Steinitz, an artist and friend who has spent much of her life sharing her knowledge and love for Leonardo da Vinci with the world.

© 1980 by Gemini Smith Inc. and Ernest Raboff

First published in Great Britain 1980 by Ernest Benn Limited
25 New Street Square, London EC4A 3JA and Sovereign Way, Tonbridge, Kent TN9 1RW

Printed in Japan by Toppan
ISBN 0 510 00102 5

Leonardo da Vinci by Ernest Raboff

Art for Children

A GEMINI-SMITH BOOK
EDITED BY BRADLEY SMITH

Ernest Benn
LONDON & TONBRIDGE

LEONARDO DA VINCI was born on 15th April, 1452 in Vinci, a quiet mountain village about a day's journey by mule cart from Florence in Italy. He was the illegitimate son of Ser Piero da Vinci, a successful notary who later moved to Florence where he was employed by the powerful, ruling Medici family. All that is known about his mother is that she was almost certainly of noble birth and that her name was Caterina.

His childhood was carefree and happy and he grew into a gifted and handsome youth. He was so handsome that later when he walked in the streets of Florence people would stop to look at him. By the age of seventeen he was working and studying in the studio of the famous painter Andrea del Verrocchio.

Having the advantage of being the son of a wealthy father, Leonardo never had to struggle for a living and his gifts were so extraordinary that his reputation was established from the very beginning. He has been described as 'the complete Renaissance man'.

The Virgin of the Rocks   National Gallery, London

The Renaissance, which means 'rebirth', was a time of immense enthusiasm for ideas and their development in both the arts and sciences. No subject was beyond Leonardo's ability or beneath his concern; for him knowledge and beauty were one and the same thing.

As a musician he invented new instruments and adapted existing ones. He wrote extensively on the theory, study and practice of music. He composed. He wrote songs. He was a virtuoso performer, famed for the sweetness of his voice and his improvisations on the lyre. He became renowned as an engineer, architect, mathematician, philosopher, sculptor and painter. He studied and mastered anatomy, even himself dissecting human corpses in his determination to understand. He studied botany. He analysed the movement of water. He loved and admired animals, especially horses, and often drew, painted and sculpted them. As an inventor he still astonishes us with the depth of his perception and the quality of his originality.

As well as being a man of extraordinary genius, he was also a man of kindness, humour and compassion. He was an optimist too, believing in the goodness of life and that it had a purpose. 'Man is not born to mourn in idleness but to work at large and magnificent tasks, thereby pleasing and honouring God and manifesting in himself *perfect virtù*, that is, the fruit of happiness.'

Leonardo was driven by a passion to learn all the arts and all the sciences. It was said by his contemporaries that heaven had bestowed on him its most heavenly gifts; the difficulty was which of his many talents he would pursue in order to master them. At the end of his life, it could also be said of him that he had discovered more and learned more than anyone before him.

In 1516, King Francis I invited Leonardo to live in France. He spent his remaining years there in the Palace de Choix near Amboise and died on 2nd May, 1519.

Self-portrait Royal Library, Turin

THE LADY WITH THE ERMINE

Leonardo composed his paintings using geometric proportions as a basis of design. Renaissance painters and architects applied to their work mathematical principles discovered by the ancient Greeks whose knowledge had, until the 15th Century, almost been forgotten.

In this painting the strong, stable pyramid is the underlying form. Of course, this triangular shape is only an invisible foundation on which Leonardo builds.

Studies of Two Children Kissing
Royal Collection, Windsor

Study of Clasped Hands
Royal Collection, Windsor

Both the lady and her pet are expressed with many interrelating curved lines and planes. These curves, or arcs, commence at the apex of the pyramid in the modelling of the head. Notice the unbroken line made by the hair around forehead, cheek and jaw, sweeping into the arc of the shoulder. The sleeve of the dress follows the downward movement and then upwards again to the ermine's paw. From there our eye is taken around the animal's body to the sleeve on the opposite side and back to the starting point.

The only nearly straight lines to be seen are the thin, black circlet around the lady's brow and the square-cut neckline of her dress. Their angularity contrasts with the surrounding gentle roundness and adds a quality of dignity and strength combined.

At first sight, the elements which make up this portrait seem quite simple and straightforward. The more we look into the composition, however, the more we can appreciate the richness and subtlety of its rhythms.

Robinia   Royal Collection, Windsor

The Lady with the Ermine   Czartoryski Museum, Cracow

THE LADY WITH THE ERMINE (Detail)

The young lady has a sense of humour as well as being proud and beautiful. How delicately Leonardo suggests just the hint of a smile through the slightly upturned corners of her mouth and the sparkle in her eyes. How carefully, too, he blends colours and tones so that her complexion is perfectly smooth and clear. The rounded contours of her features are so finely modelled and tinted that the skin seems luminous even in the shadows.

Leonardo studied and mastered the subject of anatomy. He knew precisely the shape and form of the bone structure beneath the flesh. Just as geometry is the underlying basis of his design so his knowledge of the skeleton is the foundation on which he builds the living person.

Leonardo was a perfectionist. Everything in his pictures was important and each detail was treated with equal care and respect for truth.

Method for Walking on Water

Portrait of Massimiliano Sforza
Pinacoteca Ambrosiana, Milan

Study of Life Preserver

Detail: The Lady with the Ermine   Czartoryski Museum, Cracow

THE LADY WITH THE ERMINE (Detail)

The lady's hand and slender fingers again reveal Leonardo's understanding of anatomy. Hands are perhaps the most difficult part of the body to draw or paint convincingly. Notice that the quality of the bottom two fingers is inferior to the top two. At a much later date they were repainted by an unknown restorer.

Folly   Royal Collection, Windsor

In the portrait of the ermine Leonardo expresses with the lightest and finest of brush strokes the soft and silvery texture of the creature's fur. Underneath his coat though, the muscles are hard and taut, ready for instant action.

Unlike his mistress who looks away, the ermine gazes suspiciously out at us with hard bright eyes. His posture is alert, but still, with a paw raised and held in mid-air. His ears are cocked and listening for the slightest sounds. It is easy to believe that in ancient times ermines were kept as mouse-catchers instead of cats. Just like a cat, he will stay on his owner's lap only as long as it suits him.

In this painting Leonardo completely captures the lithe strength, fierce energy and independence of this beautiful little predator.

The Crab   Wallraf-Richartz Museum, Cologne

The Mouse and the Cat   Royal Collection, Windsor

Detail: The Lady with the Ermine   Czartoryski Museum, Cracow

MONA LISA

The *Mona Lisa,* also called *La Gioconda,* is without doubt the most famous portrait in the world. Researchers remain uncertain of her identity. Although it has long been thought she may have been the wife of a wealthy silk merchant, it now seems likely she was Isabella of Aragon, the widowed Duchess of Milan.

Time has cracked the paintwork and many layers of varnish have dimmed the colour but, still, she retains her strange power. Her features and their expression have an unearthly quality and defy analysis. The beautiful and mysterious face haunts the imagination of everyone who sees it.

Intemperance   British Museum, London

Her posture is simple and graceful. Her hands rest quietly and calmly across one another on the arm of the chair in which she is seated. Jagged mountains rising from still waters loom behind her in a distant landscape. The deep blues and greens in this background contrast with the warm glowing flesh tones of her face, breast and hands. Every strand of hair falling to her shoulders, every fold in the garments she wears and each stitch in the embroidered neckline is perfectly realised.

Sketches: Studies for Madonna with Cat   British Museum, London

Mona Lisa   The Louvre, Paris

MONA LISA (Detail)

In this detail of the *Mona Lisa* we can study her expression more closely.

The eyes seem to gaze directly at us and at the same time, past us and, though smiling, there is a hint of sadness in them too. They seem to be asking a mysterious question whilst, also, looking inwards to secret thoughts.

The beautiful bird-wing curve of the eyebrows is echoed in the delicate shape of the nostrils and below them in the tender smile. The muscles of the smooth cheeks are rounded by this smile and stretch upwards from the corners of the lips to meet the corners of the eyes.

The more we look, the more we appreciate the perfection of her features. Through them, Leonardo expresses qualities of gentleness, humour, serenity, nobility and mystery. So alive and real is this portrait, it is difficult to believe that it was painted over 450 years ago. Only the paintwork, cracked like crazing on an old china bowl, reminds us of its antiquity.

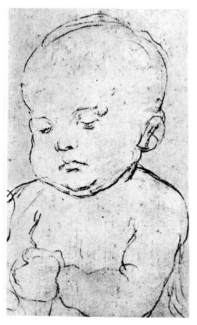

Head of Child   Uffizi Gallery, Florence

**Postures of Babies, Studies for Fresco
Royal Collection, Windsor**

Detail: Mona Lisa   The Louvre, Paris

ST. ANNE, THE VIRGIN AND THE INFANT CHRIST WITH A LAMB

In this picture the infant Jesus holds a lamb which is a symbol of himself. He is often called 'the lamb of God'. Lambs were sometimes sacrificed as an offering to God and from the New Testament we know that Jesus, as a grown man, was to die on the cross to save mankind.

Just as Leonardo shows a connection between Jesus and the lamb he links the Virgin and her son in the same way. Their two pairs of arms are literally links in a chain. From above the Virgin Mother, St. Anne smiles down with loving approval.

The feeling of quiet joy in the picture comes from the gently smiling faces and the relaxed, graceful postures of the figures. The composition though is strong, with bold curving rhythms beginning with the lamb's tail and continuing upwards through the outstretched arms above. Notice how the line across the Virgin's shoulder and neck sweeps into the jutting elbow and separates St. Anne's head from the rest of the design. In this way Leonardo sets her a little apart and at the same time allows her head, at the top of the pyramid of figures, to crown the composition.

In the foreground the red-brown colours and the dark silhouetted tree are very much in this world. In the background the strange, ethereal mountains seem more heavenly than earthly.

Drawing for St. Anne   The Louvre, Paris

Kneeling Woman   British Museum

St. Anne, The Virgin and the Infant Christ with a Lamb   The Louvre, Paris

Feminine Headdress
Royal Collection, Windsor

ST. ANNE, THE VIRGIN AND THE INFANT CHRIST WITH A LAMB (Detail)

St. Anne is not only set apart from the other figures by the composition. Her downcast inward-looking eyes and the darker flesh tones of her face emphasise the feeling of separateness. Light does not seem to shine so strongly on her as it does on the Virgin, the infant Jesus and the lamb. She is simply content to be present with those she loves and to share in the meaning of their lives.

Love is also expressed in the Virgin's face but mixed with sadness. She knows what will one day happen to her son and the pain she must bear because of it.

In this detail we can clearly see some of the curving rhythms of the composition mentioned on the previous page. The bold arc of the Virgin's shoulder rises from the pleated material of the sleeve on one side and, on the other, flows around the face back into the neck.

Young Woman   Former Royal Collection, Turin

Detail: St. Anne, The Virgin and the Infant Christ with a Lamb   The Louvre, Paris

ST. ANNE, THE VIRGIN AND THE INFANT CHRIST WITH A LAMB (Detail)

In this detail, Leonardo expresses the qualities of gentleness and innocence.

The Christ Child turns his head to smile up at his mother. His arms are outstretched just as hers are. The lamb, his ears firmly held, gazes upwards too. His sad, patient face, shaped like an arrow, points in the direction our eyes must follow. The infant seems to be showing the lamb to his mother and asking her a question.

The child and the lamb together seem to be illuminated by a single, gentle spotlight which catches and emphasises the smooth rounded flesh of the one and the soft, woolly contours of the other. This circle of light draws them close together and Leonardo further connects them by subtly repeating the tightly rolled curls on the child's head in the smaller loops of the fleece.

The Dog and the Flea
Royal Collection, Windsor

Ass and Ox   Royal Collection, Windsor

Detail: St. Anne, The Virgin and the Infant Christ with a Lamb   The Louvre, Paris

PORTRAIT OF A MUSICIAN

In this painting, only the face and part of the hair is completed. The rest is only roughly sketched in.

The upright, almost military, stance of the young man contrasts with the rather dreamy, faraway expression on his face. He holds a sheet of music very stiffly and 'correctly' but looks as if he had quite forgotten he was doing so.

Even though details are absent, we can see the composition well enough. The strong simple horizontals of cap, collar, hand and music sheet create a feeling of stability and dignity. The curved diagonals of the hair and the opposing angles of the two broad strips of material add force and movement.

Light strikes the face from the front revealing the clear modelling of the features. Again we can appreciate how well Leonardo understood the bone structure beneath the flesh.

Caps and Helmets   Royal Coll., Windsor

Study of Peasant Digging   Royal Coll., Windsor

Studies of Heads   Former Royal Coll., Turin

Portrait of a Musician   Pinacoteca Ambrosiana, Milan

FEMALE PORTRAIT

This lady, unlike the other paintings of women shown so far, has a serious, brooding expression on her face. Notice the small cast of one of her eyes which helps to create this withdrawn look. Her left eye gazes directly at us but the right one appears to see past us.

The modelling of her features between the two crescent shapes of hair is as fine and smooth as marble. Her skin, delicately toned and pale, is luminously contrasted against the foliage behind. This foliage, like a dark halo, completely frames her head and neck and on one side descends to the bottom of the picture. Perhaps Leonardo chose the spiky linear form of the leaves to emphasise the marble smoothness of the lady's complexion.

In the distance behind her left shoulder, we glimpse the kind of dreamlike and mysterious landscape Leonardo loved to paint. Although the tall trees with their slender stems, the water with its reflections and the misty outlines of buildings are real enough, we feel that this country is perhaps in another world.

It is now known that sometime in the past, the lower portion of the canvas was cut away. No one painted hands as beautifully as Leonardo and it is in the lost area that they would have appeared.

Drawing for St. Anne   Royal Coll., Windsor

Profile of Youth   Royal Collection, Windsor

Female Portrait   National Gallery, Washington

Group of Dancers for Allegorical Composition Academy, Venice

PORTRAIT OF A YOUNG WOMAN

This profile seems to have been painted as much to display the circlet, hair net and necklace, as to achieve a likeness of the sitter. It is believed that Leonardo almost certainly designed the beautiful jewellery himself. The circlet around the brow is made of gold and the net, of gold and pearls. He would also have designed the exquisite interlaced ornament over the shoulder.

He captures in the young woman's face a person of character with a sense of humour. As in *Lady with the Ermine* he hints at the beginnings of a smile. Unlike *Lady with the Ermine* though, her features are less than perfect and much more down to earth. Her chin and jaw are plump, her mouth full and her nose upturned. Her gaze is steady and level and there is a wordly-wise look in her eye.

Some art experts believe that parts of this picture were not actually painted by Leonardo. The background for instance is uncharacteristic of his work. It is without detail, almost black, and completely lacks his subtlety. So dark is this background colour that the shape of the back of the head and the outline of the shoulder are almost lost.

Portrait of a Young Woman   Pinacoteca Ambrosiana, Milan

THE ANNUNCIATION (Detail)

The angel, holding a lily, a symbol of purity, is telling the Virgin Mary that she is to become the mother of Christ.

The composition of the painting is divided into two equal parts by the open, or negative, space of the distant landscape, an enlarged detail of which is shown at the beginning of this book. With this separation, Leonardo seems to imply that the two figures, though together for a moment, in fact live in separate worlds; the one in heaven and the other on earth. The shapes in between, and defined by, two or more objects are called negative spaces. In any composition these areas are just as important as the objects themselves.

The very wide rectangle makes us 'read' the picture from left to right as we read a book. Our eye follows the graceful 'S' curve made by the angel's wing and the raised arm and then leaps across the dividing space to the outstretched hand of the seated Virgin. Notice the way the angel's wings, head and arm 'gather up' the trees behind and how the diagonal thrust of the kneeling posture adds a feeling of urgency.

The gentle animation of the figures contrasts with the dignity and serenity of their surroundings. The strong verticals of the trees resting on the horizontal, flower-filled bands and the wide, airy spaces express stability and tranquillity.

Each flower in its exquisite detail, each tree with its distinctive foliage and every feather on the angel's wing, reveals Leonardo's deep understanding of their individual nature and form. Leonardo's sketch books contain many examples of searching drawings of plants and trees and marvellously precise analytical studies of birds at rest and in flight.

Head and Shoulders of Warrior in Profile
British Museum

Detail: The Annunciation

The Annunciation   Uffizi Gallery, Florence

Studies and Positions of Cats   Royal Collection, Windsor